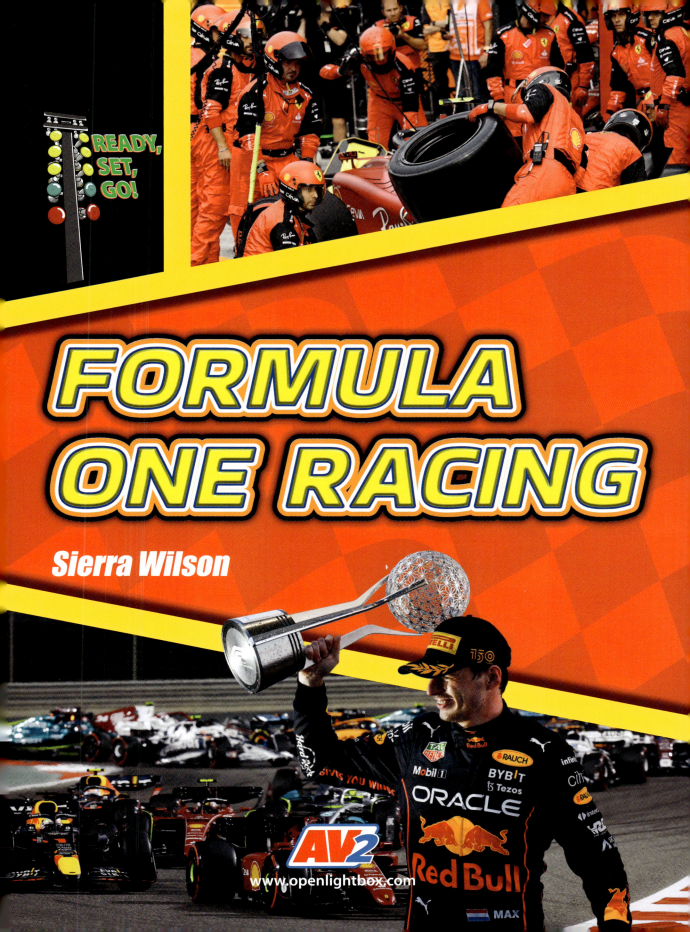

Step 1
Go to www.openlightbox.com

Step 2
Enter this unique code

AVQ36746

Step 3
Explore your interactive eBook!

AV2 is optimized for use on any device

Your interactive eBook comes with...

Contents
Browse a live contents page to easily navigate through resources

Audio
Listen to sections of the book read aloud

Videos
Watch informative video clips

Weblinks
Gain additional information for research

Slideshows
View images and captions

Try This!
Complete activities and hands-on experiments

Key Words
Study vocabulary, and complete a matching word activity

Quizzes
Test your knowledge

Share
Share titles within your Learning Management System (LMS) or Library Circulation System

Citation
Create bibliographical references following APA, CMOS, and MLA styles

This title is part of our AV2 digital subscription

1-Year Grades K–5 Subscription
ISBN 978-1-7911-3320-7

Access hundreds of AV2 titles with our digital subscription. Sign up for a FREE trial at www.openlightbox.com/trial

The digital components of this book are guaranteed to stay active for at least five years from the date of publication.

FORMULA ONE RACING

CONTENTS

- 2   Interactive eBook Code
- 4   What Is Formula One?
- 6   History of Formula One
- 8   Formula One Rules
- 10 Formula One Cars
- 12 Parts of a Formula One Car
- 14 Developing Formula One Cars
- 16 Red Bull Racing RB19
- 18 Formula One Stars
- 20 Formula One Records
- 22 Quiz
- 23 Key Words/Index

What Is Formula One?

Formula One, also known as Formula 1 or F1, is the highest level of **single-seater** car racing in the world. F1 races, called Grand Prix, are held around the globe. The 2024 and 2025 F1 seasons are the longest on record, with 24 Grand Prix held in 21 countries.

Car racing has been a popular sport since the early 1900s, and its fan base has grown steadily over time. Today, more than 1.5 billion people around the world tune in to watch the F1 season every year. F1 drivers are considered celebrities, while F1 cars are seen as symbols of innovation and excellence in **engineering**.

TRACKS AROUND THE WORLD

CIRCUIT OF THE AMERICAS (COTA)

UNITED STATES

Located outside Austin, Texas, COTA hosts several motorsports events, including **MotoGP** and **NASCAR**. It has been used for F1 racing since 2012. The track is 3.41 miles (5.49 km) long.

CIRCUIT DE MONACO

MONACO

This 2.07-mile (3.33-km) **circuit** is set up on the streets of Monte Carlo, a district of Monaco. It hosted its first race in 1929. The Monaco Grand Prix has been held here every year without interruption since 1955.

YAS MARINA CIRCUIT

UNITED ARAB EMIRATES (UAE)

The Yas Marina Circuit is in Abu Dhabi, the capital city of UAE. This track has been an F1 venue since it opened in 2009. It is 3.28 miles (5.28 km) long and can host up to 50,000 spectators.

FORMULA ONE RACING

History of Formula One

The first Grand Prix were held in France in the early 1900s. Often held on open roads, these races were dangerous to the drivers and the audience. The Fédération Internationale de l'Automobile (FIA) was established in 1904 to regulate races, increase safety, and ensure fair racing. This organization continues to oversee different motorsports around the world.

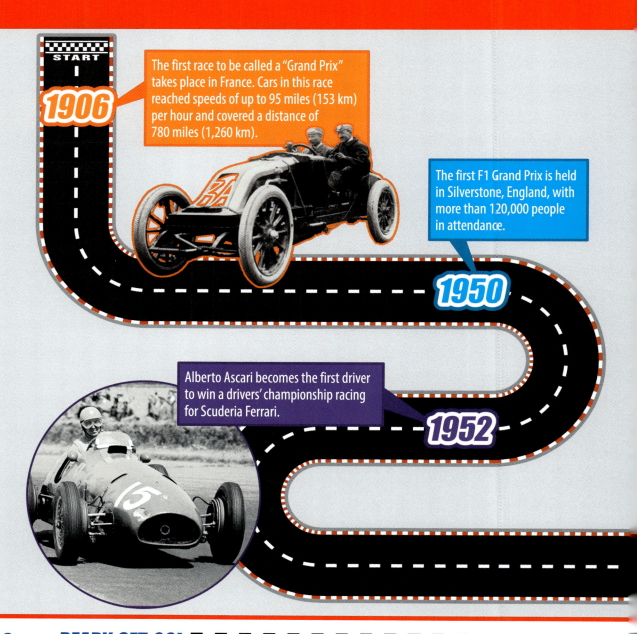

1906 — The first race to be called a "Grand Prix" takes place in France. Cars in this race reached speeds of up to 95 miles (153 km) per hour and covered a distance of 780 miles (1,260 km).

1950 — The first F1 Grand Prix is held in Silverstone, England, with more than 120,000 people in attendance.

1952 — Alberto Ascari becomes the first driver to win a drivers' championship racing for Scuderia Ferrari.

6 READY, SET, GO!

In 1949, the FIA officially created Formula One as an international championship. The first F1 season, held one year later, only included seven Grand Prix. All except one were held in Europe. In 1953, Argentina hosted South America's first F1 championship race. Five years later, the first African Grand Prix was held in Morocco. The 1976 Japanese Grand Prix was the first F1 race in Asia. Today, Grand Prix are held on five different continents.

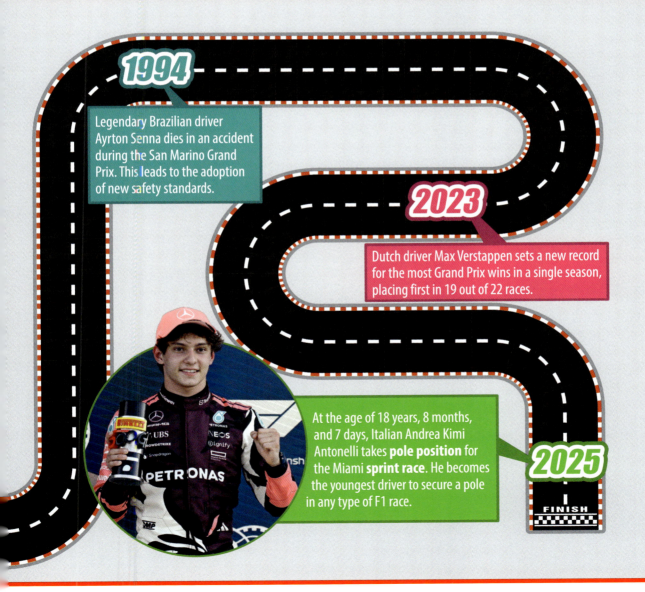

1994
Legendary Brazilian driver Ayrton Senna dies in an accident during the San Marino Grand Prix. This leads to the adoption of new safety standards.

2023
Dutch driver Max Verstappen sets a new record for the most Grand Prix wins in a single season, placing first in 19 out of 22 races.

2025
At the age of 18 years, 8 months, and 7 days, Italian Andrea Kimi Antonelli takes **pole position** for the Miami **sprint race**. He becomes the youngest driver to secure a pole in any type of F1 race.

FORMULA ONE RACING 7

Formula One Rules

To increase excitement and action, the FIA introduced sprint races to some Grand Prix weekends in 2021. In the 2025 season, six weekends featured this type of short race.

8 READY, SET, GO!

All F1 events include five sessions. There are typically three free practice sessions, a qualifying session, and the Grand Prix race. Sprint races and their qualifying sessions replace two of the practice sessions in some of the events. Almost all Grand Prix races need to be at least 190 miles (306 km) long. This means that every Grand Prix consists of a different number of laps that need to be completed around the racetrack.

The Monaco Grand Prix is the only race shorter than 190 miles (300 km). Drivers race 78 laps here, for a total of about 160 miles (260 km).

Teams are also called constructors. Ten teams, each with two drivers, compete in a Grand Prix race. Only drivers who finish in the top 10 receive points, with the winner earning 25 points and the 10th-place driver receiving 1 point. Constructors are awarded the same number of points as their drivers, based on their finishing positions. At the end of the season, the driver and constructor with the most points are crowned champions.

F1 Grand Prix Weekend

FRIDAY The first day of a Grand Prix weekend focuses on practice, with two 1-hour-long practice sessions. These sessions are designed to test the car on the racetrack. They help drivers and make adjustments to the car to suit the different features of each track.

SATURDAY The second day starts with a third practice session. In the afternoon, drivers compete against each other in the qualification event. The results of this event determine the driver order at the beginning of the Grand Prix, with the fastest driver obtaining pole position. Drivers that set the slowest time in qualifying start will start the Grand Prix at the back of the track.

SUNDAY The Grand Prix race is usually held on Sunday. Each race lasts about 2 hours. Teams provide strategic support by making decisions regarding the car's settings and the timing of **pit stops**. All decisions are communicated to a driver by his race engineer. Teams select one race engineer to maintain radio contact with each driver throughout the race.

FORMULA ONE RACING   9

Formula One Cars

In 2021, the FIA introduced a cost cap to give all teams a fair shot. The cost cap determines the maximum amount a team can spend to develop their car for the season.

F1 cars are the fastest type of road-racing cars. They do not resemble passenger cars seen on roads. F1 cars are usually very low, with a single seat and no roof. They have open wheels and wide tires that help them grip the road.

Careful design helps F1 cars remain stable even at high speeds. The car's shape is geared toward reducing **air resistance** and increasing **downforce**. The wing-like structures on F1 cars allow them to maneuver at high speeds. Each team works on developing the fastest car while adhering to FIA regulations for safety and fair racing.

It takes only **2.6 seconds** for an F1 car to reach a speed of **60 miles** (97 km) per hour.

F1 cars can go faster than **220 miles** (354 km) per hour.

Light and fast, F1 cars weigh about **half** as much as NASCAR cars.

The cost cap for the **2026** season is set at **$215 million**.

FORMULA ONE RACING

Parts of a Formula One Car

Formula One cars are carefully designed for maximum performance. Teams of engineers and designers work together to make incredibly fast cars.

Team mechanics ensure that every part of the car is in good condition for racing at high speeds. Trained to work quickly, they service the car in the shortest time possible during race pit stops.

1. FRONT WING
The front wing is the front piece of an F1 car. It is carefully designed to manage **airflow**. A good front wing will make an F1 car faster and more **aerodynamic**.

2. CHASSIS
The chassis is the skeleton of a car. Everything is connected to the chassis. It provides the basic frame and shape of an F1 car.

3. REAR WING
The rear wing is the back piece of an F1 car. The rear wing can move in order to reduce **drag** and increase speed.

4. ENGINE
An F1 car engine often provides more than 1,000 **horsepower**. F1 regulations include strict engine requirements for all cars, including the type of fuel they can use.

FORMULA ONE RACING

F1 teams rely on many different specialized professionals to develop their racing cars. Hundreds of designers, engineers, mechanics, and other skilled workers contribute to the team's efforts.

READY, SET, GO!

Developing Formula One Cars

F1 cars push the limits of car technology. Engineers and designers work together to test and develop new features to make F1 cars faster, safer, and better at racing.

Team principals, such as James Vowles of Williams Racing, lead F1 teams. They are responsible for managing both trackside operations and car development at the factory.

ENGINEERING DESIGN

IDENTIFYING CHALLENGES
Engineering teams focus on a specific problem or area for improvement. They must work within the strict guidelines and regulations set out for F1 cars.

TESTING IDEAS
Teams study and explore possible solutions. They pay special attention to the science of aerodynamics. They use math and 3D computer models to test ideas.

FINDING SOLUTIONS
After design concepts are **refined**, life-sized models are constructed and tested in **wind tunnels**. The test results allow engineers to gather information about their design and further improve their work.

FORMULA ONE RACING   15

Red Bull Racing RB19

Max Verstappen achieved a 10-race winning streak in the RB19 during the 2023 season. This broke the previous record of nine consecutive wins that was secured in 2013 by former Red Bull Racing driver Sebastian Vettel.

In 2023, the Red Bull Racing team came out with the RB19, a car that seemed unstoppable. Drivers Max Verstappen and Sergio Perez drove the RB19 throughout the season. Together, they won 21 out of the 22 races, dominating nearly every event.

Adrian Newey left Red Bull Racing in 2024. He joined Aston Martin with a record $200 million contract over five years.

The **chief technical officer** behind the RB19, Adrian Newey, had worked with Red Bull Racing for 19 years. His work on the RB19 helped the team break many records, including the one for the most points scored by a team in a season. Red Bull finished the 2023 season with 860 points, winning the constructors' championship for that year. Their score was more than double that of Mercedes AMG Petronas, the second-place finisher.

Top Three Finishes
30

Power Output
900 horsepower

Weight
331 pounds
(150 kilograms)

Wins in 2023
21

RB19

Points in 2023
860

FORMULA ONE RACING

Formula One Stars

Lewis Hamilton

Birth: 1985, Stevenage, England

Teams: McLaren, Mercedes AMG Petronas, Scuderia Ferrari

Years Active: 2007 to present

Lewis Hamilton began racing remote-controlled cars as a young child and moved to **go-kart** racing soon after. Today, many people consider him the greatest F1 driver of all time. He holds the records for most wins, pole positions, and total career points, and has been crowned the drivers' champion seven times.

18 READY, SET, GO!

Michael Schumacher

Birth: 1969, Cologne, Germany

Teams: Jordan, Benetton, Scuderia Ferrari, Mercedes AMG Petronas

Years Active: 1991 to 2006 and 2010 to 2012

Michael Schumacher began his career as a go-kart racer, starting on a track managed by his father. He quickly became a skilled and passionate racer, widely regarded as one of the best of all time. Along with Lewis Hamilton, Schumacher is one of only two drivers to have won seven drivers' championships.

Max Verstappen

Birth: 1997, Hasselt, Belgium

Teams: Toro Rosso, Red Bull

Years Active: 2015 to present

The son of a former F1 driver, Max Verstappen began racing go-karts when he was only 4 years old. At just 17, he became the youngest F1 driver in history. Verstappen won four consecutive F1 drivers' championships between 2021 and 2024.

FORMULA ONE RACING

Formula One Records

7 Championships
Most World Championships Won by a Single Driver
Both Lewis Hamilton and Michael Schumacher secured seven championship wins.

16 Championships
Constructor with the Most World Championship Wins
Ferrari won the championship 16 times between 1961 and 2007.

231.4 Mph
Fastest Speed in an F1 Race
In 2016, Valtteri Bottas set the record speed of 231.4 miles (372.4 km) per hour driving for Williams Mercedes.

READY, SET, GO!

105 Wins
Most F1 Grand Prix Wins
Lewis Hamilton won 105 races between 2008 and 2024.

Most Consecutive Pole Positions
Ayrton Senna started eight races in a row on pole between 1988 and 1989. Max Verstappen tied this record in between 2023 and 2024.

8 Pole Positions

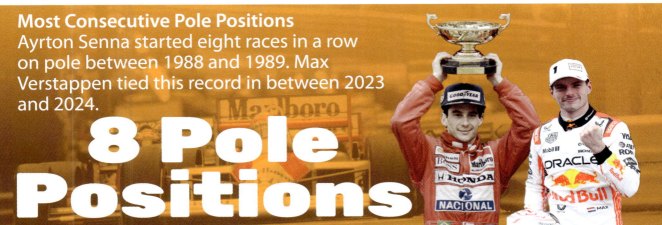

1.8 Seconds

Fastest Pit Stop
In 2023, McLaren's pit crew completed a pit stop in 1.8 seconds.

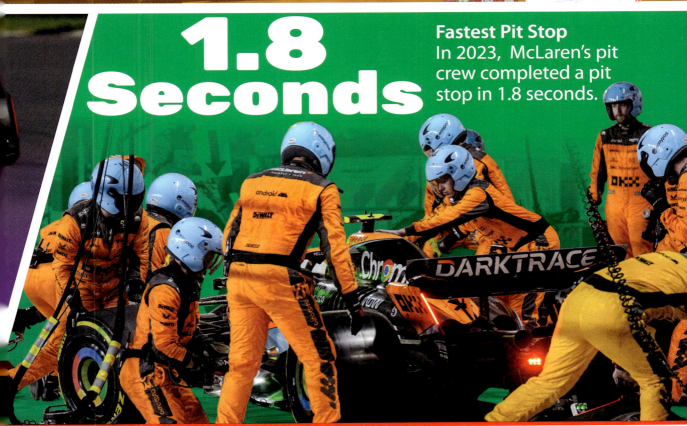

FORMULA ONE RACING

Quiz

1. Where was the first F1 Grand Prix held in 1950?
2. What is the record for the fastest pit stop in an F1 race?
3. Which country is Michael Schumacher from?
4. Who achieved a record 10-win streak during the 2023 season?
5. When was the FIA founded?
6. What is the name of the front piece of an F1 car?
7. How much is the cost cap for the 2026 season?
8. Who holds the records for the most Grand Prix wins?
9. Which part of an F1 car is like the car's skeleton?
10. At what age did Andrea Kimi Antonelli become the youngest driver to secure a pole position?

ANSWERS: **1.** Silverstone, England **2.** 1.8 seconds **3.** Germany **4.** Max Verstappen **5.** 1904 **6.** The front wing **7.** $215 million **8.** Lewis Hamilton **9.** The chassis **10.** 18 years, 8 months, and 7 days

22 — READY, SET, GO!

Key Words

aerodynamic: related to the ability to move smoothly through the air

airflow: the motion and direction of air

air resistance: the force that pushes against an object moving through air

chief technical officer: the person responsible for overseeing the design, development, and technical performance of an F1 team's car

circuit: a closed track where races are held

downforce: the force that pushes a car down onto the track to help it grip the road and stay stable, especially at high speeds

drag: the force that opposes the motion of an object through air

engineering: designing and building the technical parts of a car using math and science

go-kart: a small racing car with four wheels and no roof, often used by beginners to practice racing

horsepower: a unit of power used to measure the engine's ability to produce force

MotoGP: the top-level motorcycle racing series, where the best riders race high-performance motorcycles on various tracks around the world

NASCAR: a popular American racing series featuring stock cars

pit stops: brief stops during a race for the car to get repairs, new tires, or fuel

pole position: the starting spot at the front of the grid, earned by the driver with the fastest qualifying time

refined: improved by making small changes

single-seater: a type of race car with just one seat for the driver

sprint race: a 62-mile (100-km) race held on Saturdays at some F1 events, with points awarded to the fastest eight drivers

wind tunnels: large tubes that have air flowing inside and are used to test the aerodynamics of vehicles

Antonelli, Andrea Kimi 7, 8, 22
Ascari, Alberto 6

Bottas, Valtteri 20

chief technical officer 17
Circuit de Monaco 5
Circuit of the Americas (COTA) 5
cost cap 10, 11, 22

engineering 4, 9, 12, 14, 15

Fédération Internationale de l'Automobile (FIA) 6, 7, 10, 11, 22

Hamilton, Lewis 8, 18, 19, 20, 21, 22

McLaren 21
mechanics 12, 14
Mercedes AMG Petronas 8, 17, 18, 19

Newey, Adrian 17

RB19 16, 17
Red Bull Racing 16, 17, 19

Schumacher, Michael 19, 20, 22
Scuderia Ferrari 6, 8, 18, 19, 20
Senna, Ayrton 7, 21
sprint race 7, 8, 9

team principals 15

Verstappen, Max 7, 16, 17, 19, 21, 22
Vowles, James 15

Williams Racing 15, 20

Yas Marina Circuit 5

FORMULA ONE RACING 23

Get the best of both worlds.

AV2 bridges the gap between print and digital.

The expandable rescurces toolbar enables quick access to content including **videos**, **audio**, **activities**, **weblinks**, **slideshows**, **quizzes**, and **key words**.

Animated videos make static images come alive.

Resource icons on each page help readers to further **explore key concepts**.

Published by Lightbox Learning Inc.
276 5th Avenue, Suite 704 #917
New York, NY 10001
Website: www.openlightbox.com

Copyright ©2026 Lightbox Learning Inc.
All rights reserved. No part of this publication may be reproduced, stored in a retrieval system, or transmitted in any form or by any means, electronic, mechanical, photocopying, recording, or otherwise, without the prior written permission of the publisher.

Library of Congress Control Number: 2025940636

ISBN 979-8-8745-0390-1 (hardcover)
ISBN 979-8-8745-0391-8 (softcover)
ISBN 979-8-8745-0710-7 (static multi-user eBook)
ISBN 979-8-8745-0392-5 (interactive multi-user eBook)

062025
101124

Printed in the United States of America in Fargo, North Dakota
1 2 3 4 5 6 7 8 9 0 29 28 27 26 25

Project Coordinator: Sara Cucini   Designer: Mandy Christiansen   Layout: Jean Faye Rodriguez

The publisher has made every reasonable effort to trace ownership of and to obtain permission to use copyright material. The publisher would be pleased to have any errors or omissions brought to its attention so that they may be corrected in subsequent printings. Some visual elements in this title may have been generated using AI. While we strive for accuracy in all aspects of our products, we cannot guarantee that the elements depicted in these images are accurate. The publisher acknowledges Getty Images and Alamy as the primary image suppliers for this title. If you have any inquiries about these images or would like to provide any feedback, please reach out to us at feedback@openlightbox.com

All of the Internet URLs and Google Maps links given in the interactive eBook were valid at the time of publication. However, due to the dynamic nature of the Internet, some addresses may have changed, or sites may have ceased to exist since publication. While the author and publisher regret any inconvenience this may cause readers, no responsibility for any such changes can be accepted by either the author or the publisher.

View new titles and product videos at **www.openlightbox.com**